LOVE, Poems of Longing

LOVE
Poems of Longing

Copyright © 2016 by Nikos Linardakis and Light Book Publishers. All Rights Reserved. Printed in the United States of America. No part of this book may be used or reproduced in any manner whatsoever without written permission except in the case of reprints in the context of reviews.

Light Book Publishers

www.LightBookPublishers.com

16 17 18 19 20   10 9 8 7 6 5 4 3 2 1

FIRST EDITION

ISBN: 978-1-884084-06-5

This book is a work of fiction. Names, characters, places, and incidents either are products of the author's imagination or are used fictitiously. Any resemblance to actual events or locales or persons, living or dead, is entirely coincidental.

Cover Photograph and Illustrations by Nikos Linardakis

In loving memory of my father, Dr. Mike,
and my caring mother, Lambrini.

Dedication

I couple my hands,
    To thoughts of good,
    Embraced in time,
    Affinity.

For here is my poetry,
    Tremors abound,
    But now are steady,
    My parents, my ground.

LOVE
Poems of Longing

by

Nikos Linardakis

Preface

Poems have always been identified with some form of Love. Poetry is a sequence of creative thought, and builds an intimacy between the poet, the reader and life. I wish to provide such an intimate bond, so that maybe, just maybe, *one* poem in this book warms your heart and moves your soul.

The poems were written in no dedicated style or form, a few may rhyme, but most are presented as open poems, as rough, passionate insights to the intensity of human moments. The words are symbolic of giving and offering self-sacrifice, which is the true essence of Love.

I hope you delight in my poems and share them with others. Please cherish this art of poetry, as if we are reading together.

With grateful affection,

Nikos

April, 2016

Contents

I. **The Family**
    a. Family — 17
    b. Self-Sacrifice — 19
    c. Mother I Love You — 21
    d. The Band — 23
    e. Philotimo — 25
    f. Parents Profound — 27

II. **The Moments**
    a. Metanoia — 31
    b. Longing — 33
    c. A Moment to Meet — 35
    d. The Morning Delivery — 37
    e. Embrace Our Beauty — 39
    f. The Things We Do For Love — 41
    g. Anxious — 43
    h. I Wish You Knew — 47

III. **The Person**
    a. My Only Love — 51
    b. Finding Fulfillment — 53
    c. Love Languages — 57
    d. Loneliness — 59
    e. May You be my Good Friend — 61
    f. Constantine — 63
    g. Today I swim, Tomorrow I Dance — 65
    h. One—A Haiku Poem — 73

IV. The Life
- a. A New Beginning — 77
- b. The Fifth Season — 79
- c. Friends Pair with Intimacy — 81
- d. Soon, I See — 85
- e. Birds Without Wings — 87
- f. Become — 89
- g. La Magie de Paris — 91
- h. A Theme not Twirled — 93
- i. Love Has No Scenery — 95
- j. Opa! — 99

Part 1.

The Family

Family

Hold on to family
For if family dies
Love remains there
With many cries.

Hold on to family
For when children go
Love is anonymous
With limited glow.

Hold on to family
For when parents smile
Love captures all
And pleasant hearts pile.

Self-Sacrifice

How my mind can hold with its pain,
More fragrant is my choice to offer, instead of gain.
Put a loved one above your own,
Away with happiness, success, or even a life throne.

Love much that you are willing to lay down your life,
Or provide, while living slim, in clay and strife.
Or love a person so much that your souls ache,
With desire, can't name or blaze for future's sake.

And when it happens you will feel a glow,
That you are willing to die at that moment, and know.
Leave your last breath laying, given to love's day,
I name my life for you, at the altar our way.

Like a plan deferred, it may carry weight,
But I assure goodness will spread, without hate.
Turn your melancholy into dismay,
They cast irons of difficulty, but it will not stay.

Don't listen to thieves take over your light,
Sway only for your children and protect with might.
Don't mind what they say, instead gather and pray,
You made the self-sacrifice for this paradise I say.

Like the yeast to make bread rise,
Until the moment it opens eyes,
Then, let go of the sacrifice ties.

At that moon evening, climb out from under torment,
For love's self-sacrifice, will help find your true self.

Mother, I Love You

(This is a Greek "Mandinada" poem, and was originally written by my father in 1968. I have translated it directly as I did not want to alter the essence of his words. I include it in Greek as well, for you and for my mother.)

My Mother, I love you
This is why I watch you
Thou art my protection
And in my heart, I have you.

Every morning I awaken
And I do my cross
To God I pray
To have you on my side.

So that I may grow up quickly
So that I may help you
And dreams my mother
I shall fulfill.

Thou mother you are sleepless
And you are busy all day
You care to perfection
Everything that you bring forward.

Not just that you are tired
You do not complain to me
Your child you sense
And how happy you are.

ΜΑΝΟΥΛΑ ΜΟΥ ΣΕ ΑΓΑΠΩ

Μανουλα μου σε αγαπω
γιαυτο και σε προσεχω
συ εισαι η προστασια μου
εις την καρδια μου σ εχω.

Καθε πρωι σηκωνομαι
και κανω τον σταυρο μου
τον θεον παρακαλω
να σ εχη στο πλευρο μου.

Να μεγαλωσω γρηγορα
για να σε βοηθησω
και ονειρα μανουλα μου
να πραγματοποιησω.

Εσυ μητερα ξενυκτας
και τρεχεις ολη μερα
φροντιζεις στην εντελεια
ολα να φερης περα.

Παρ ολον που κουραζεσαι
δεν μου παραπονησαι
το παιδι σου αισθανεσαι
κι ευτυχισμενη εισαι.

The Band

Fingers slide,
Lips move,
Hearts beat,
Songs carry.
A match, a final detail—the patrons dance merry.

Listeners tied,
Scripts groove,
Charts heat,
Wrongs covey.
A catch, a thankful female—the maidens glance bravely.

Singers pride,
Waves prove,
Hearts tweet,
Songs sassy.
A latch, a civil inhale—the unions prance fancy.

Band's share,
Hips prove,
Starts feet,
Songs bounty,
A batch, an artful foxtail—the virgins stance dearly.

The piano fills with tempo and carrying eyes,
The drum plays with bongo and converging highs.
The guitar sails with credo and nurturing sighs,
The woman maze flatters and impresses with lies.
In The Band, the performer rides.
In The Band, the crazier glides.

Philotimo

He is the love of honor, the highest virtue,
Of gratitude and generosity.
For ambitious man, it is like breathing,
Of servitude and ideology.

Philotimo is here, to visit, the deist value,
Of quietude and morality.
Hero's credo is clear, plan in it, the taoist renew,
Love fortitude and bigheartedly.

Arms open to abundance,
Kind gestures in places built right with acceptance.
Charms listen to confidence,
Bind beggars in barges filled tight with misguidance.

His goodness is only known to others,
He's unaware of his kindness shared.
He's never asked and probably never will,
What would it add, but a small thrill?

Virtuoso shares satisfaction,
As a giving companion,
Appreciative of his station,
A friend of bravery says one.

Philotimo begins as love again,
In alpha thru omega,
Love of Philos and Timi,
A blend of energy rays sun.

Parents Profound

Foundation of stone, plaster and color,
They built a fortress for us to take cover.
When not feeling happy as life weighed,
Our wonderful parents struggled without say.

They stuck their method and made their pay,
Housing four children, seeing them play.
When not requiring tempo in strife dismay,
Their ethical patience battled without stray.

Grief loss, verse by father was strong,
An irreplaceable mother called in song.
A father passed in tragedy to cancer's prey,
Our Archangel Michael carried that day.

We listened in attention, as mother would say,
Do your homework, but don't play.
The children rise and called her blessed,
Kept calm with love and crawled a test.

Parents' vision in devotion will not leave you,
They make life abundant and rarely see you.
The beacon wise and tall life cast,
Take care of them gently in age and last.

Part 2.

The Moments

Metanoia

With the delight of a New Year's entrance,
Metanoia comes to mind.
How often can man be kind,
I wonder, where did this spiritual gift arise?

With the changing of a view, cheers expanse,
A new heart opens and in comes Light's trance.
In front is the sunshine, behind a shadow's stance,
My mission is blessed and God's will nears chance.

With new leadership at New Year's development,
Metanoia gives to kind.
Real action takes place beyond ears, eyes and mind.
I wonder, where does this serious man unwind?

A breaking of son's blind,
A clue part evens and skin shines with bright.
No grunt for a deadline, inclined lonely the crossbow,
My fission is expressed and God's will cheers dance.

With the limelight is a New Year's essence,
Meh-tah-NOY-ah drums away life's vengeance.
Soften can man progress, in brightness and patience,
I wonder, where did this miracle gain presence?

Metanoia,
Awakening,
Repentance,
Changing of the mind.

Longing

She replenishes the world with words and blessings.
"Joyous Romance" she says.

My heart palpitates, with new-sprung tympani.
The bass beats a yielding tone, with flowing force.

I just cannot cast a motion.
Her delicate, heated touch, it forms me.

It's her neck you see.
Affectionate and devoted is her caress.

Holding me, her hands strengthen and we jointly wrap.
An equal and communicating grip.

Another advance, now it is her warm breath.
With her moist touch, we unite in celebration.

I can breathe her in, her taste, her feel.
We have grown young and we are eighteen.

Youth I see, youth I hear, youth I feel.
Engage in me.

Breath I receive.
My organs beat, I feel hers corresponding.

Take it slow and hold me affectionately.
Passion is You
Are exquisite.

A Moment to Meet

A reminder of the meeting of souls,
A bouquet, a traditional corsage.
If it seems to have disappeared,
Remind each other, union entourage.

A moment to meet,
Bind and transform.
Into pure joy —
Kiss, fusion, freeform.

The Morning Delivery

To remember her smile and caring eyes,
But it's been several years.
Could my memory explain this kind woman,
How one day she brought me cheers.

Her name was Helen,
She smiled and introduced.
I have your book! One in a million!
I remembered and deduced.

What a doll, the explanations flew,
Overall, her recollection knew.
We shared, we laughed, we talked, we listened.
And, as quickly as it began, our end glistened.

Adio! I wavered now,
Helen was a delightful visit at Federal Express,
She formed a morning summit in orchestral finesse.
She was gracious, a princess.

Embrace our Beauty

May God's hand be in your day,
Peace and grace from our loving Father is our clay.
Simple words have led to an embrace,
Kindness and gestures make faith bond in our stay.

I come across a gentle woman of my time,
She is elegant, pleasant, and funny without wine.
We cherish each other and carry small chimes,
Are we ding-a-lings or good friends sharing rhymes?

I manage to come forward and ask for togetherness,
A passage we want and promise to harness.
We exchange sweet rings and smile for a long time,
I skittle a handful and with her gentile sunshine!

Somehow I know that things will be just right,
And I embrace her beauty, and cling on tight.
She's my princess for sure and I do know that,
We are creating a new life, with a start and her cat.

"Embrace our Beauty" is the motto for us,
Showcase our dearly; love, glee, duo, less fuss.

The Things We Do for Love

Lip Smackin'
    Finger Lickin'
        Rib Ticklin'
            Knee Slappin'
                Foot Stompin'
                    Great Tastin'!
Now that's good barbecue, That's Dickey's!

I read these words on a cup and thought to myself,
The things we do for Love…
What happens when a man meets a woman?
They have to have faith in one another.

Takin' care of business, every day,
The alarm clocks wake and we calmingly pray.
The lyra plays and strengthens away,
In peace, with determination's say.

Time to dance, a walk, a chance to become again.
The things we do for Love…

I look again at the cup, and it is true
Her lips are divine,
    I kiss her neckline,
        A caress and no deadline,
           Her body touches mine,
               We make love by design,
                  Together we are a lifeline!
Now that's good rendezvous, That's Nicky's!

The things we do for Love.

Anxious

A degree of anxiousness arrives.
Is she a good woman or not?
I only hope she doesn't have different lives.

It's been at least five years since we've met,
At coffee, tea, or a party—I have not seen her yet.
May I retract and not extend a date?
No, I must pursue her, for she is a beauty made great.

I awaken again, on day two with apprehend.
She texts to confirm, we have a date, I pretend.
Will we be good? Will we have fun?
I really hope she's not going to run!

My motorcycle starts up and off I go,
Driving in daybreak within minutes until I show.
As I arrive, my havoc begins,
I offer to sit down, and finally small wins.

She submits kindly and gestures, this is.
I don't mind it one bit as she beams with bliss.
She's so pleasant and kind,
I can hardly believe whom I'm with.

Please dear beauty, comfort me so,
Gelato I recommend, with a blanket throw,
She makes me smile and I offer more.

On another night we settled with intention,
She created a cozy dinner plan.
Occasion I kissed her, it was really the first,
I embraced this time, holding my thirst.

More than friendship, I had her in my arms,
Don't leave me tomorrow, for I want us to be.
Let me prove to my angel,
That I am more than you see.

My affection beats heartedly, I enter you slow,
I see you as my darling, but the Arranger says no.
Cleverly you option, this night will not end,
We must continue again and deliver more, I intend.

Time did shift and leave me to wonder,
Those days are but past, heart's endearing love last,
Each month with full moon, cuddles embrace you,
My lovely from youth, charm holds and delights thru.

As this warm flirtation came to term,
We decided to drift dear, and climb up to learn.
I held her hand with no fear, and let friendship return,
She was my darling sweetheart, my moon's yearn.

I Wish You Knew

Something tells me you always knew,
Everything about pause was clue,
Whenever we met it seemed I'd collapse,
In that moment, it was happenstance.

Yet our timing was off and sort of seemed,
You thought and used a compass for treasures,
We worked hard, endured life's pleasures,
But our beaming showoff did not ever join.

I wish you knew, my heart paused,
I adored you with all flaws.
Every time I saw you, you made me free,
I wish you knew, oh how much, I love thee.

Part 3.

The Person

My Only Love

You've heard this once before,
But love has more than to forget,
Where else less seldom does man fret,
But love deeper than ships down wet.

In battles did men win,
Less or more than alive begin,
As energy converts from voice to choir,
More frequent love mutates from good to dire.

So let me say this straight and strong:
I love Maria as my mate, we belong.
My duty is to last and protect love's truth,
It's higher and mightier than the sky or my youth.

With God chose us, a pair centillion and wiser,
My only Love, my life companion and lover.
Let me take 'till death and to our last breath,
My only Love, my life, my passion and flower.

The heavens grateful with the answer,
And the answers with the question.
The sides don't weaken bricks character,
Myth in Crete affection.

Earning in this world is battle,
Tall kings must resign.
In one ancestor's bearing struggle,
Why did we do fine?
Because our only love, we protect,
Applause agapi love, we respect.

Finding Fulfillment

For time is a precious commodity,
We must carefully beware,
Seeking our true path,
So, we don't lead into another despair!

Happiness abounds with goodness around,
Even in sadness, there is kindness to be found.
We can overcome obstacles, clever we are,
Just jump into work, and we know we go far!

Creativity makes sense,
It brings great impact on life's collisions,
It frees us to do good,
When we may only see the bad.

Good spirits and inspiration,
Bring us closer to each other,
The kids seem to have fun,
And our families may be another.

Because of ambition,
I'm not worried of anything difficult,
She cools even in the heat, all worried for defeat,
I console to stay calm, all good, with plenty to eat!

We have one true life, and we need it to grow,
How we dance in the moonlight, tells me it will flow.
This unstoppable force, its path we may not know,
From above I can sense, it is kind and will glow.

The weather in the fall season is perfect,
We grasp it with love,
I await her each day to feel her warm body,
I can't help but want to be in it all day!

Each step we take together,
Fulfillment I see,
We can ask questions and more later,
Or build a life actually.

Our potential has begun,
It is inspired,
I'm writing and I know it will be done,
Our true course is now being spun.

I welcome our time together,
We practice with each other each day,
Our chemistry is perfect,
She's so lovely, I kiss her right away!

My dreams have always followed my knowledge,
Costs in climbing it may,
With her, I sense peace and harmony,
Together we will stay.

Finding fulfillment is a road for enlightenment,
Destination may not be something to seek,
As we may be at home,
With as little as embracing her hand, to feel complete.

I know this kind person,
She is scrumptious and hard working,
Destiny happens unplanned,
She is luscious and hand keeping.

Love Languages

Maria,
The name of Mar, the Star of the Sea,
Beloved and wished,
I love thee!

Utopia,
I'm aloft with heart of glee,
Nourished and kissed,
My soul's bakery.

Fantasia,
Blue apron meals oui,
Cherished and missed,
Of leisure's free.

Señora,
Our love languages key,
Relished and nourished,
My soul's chastity.

Have I told you?
How much you mean to me,
Your woman's touch and gentleness,
I love thee!

Loneliness

When did my loneliness begin to frown,
Where should it leave me drown,
Why would I let my heart down?

These autumn cannons, strong and gray
The ward with crippled marriage groan
The snubs and sleaze
No alley flings of grapevine breastbone
And candid shortages.

Rinse thirst you, brewing, sprawled my banquet yours
Deem brandy, and the sadness pours
Calm, sway, dew, stay
And insincere ethos this smear matures
Tissue, flex, beer, frappe.

Now if these urges dare send to stove
And give the awning weaves above
And sleep new gem
Grey beam to stall anxiously from above
Strike to a stratagem.

Charging in one with the abandoned dangers
Dry cup the constant words in errors
Fine in the eye
And all the pleasant of the archangel towers
Spurns milieu anxiously.

Then did my loneliness begin to drown,
Where should it leave me frown,
Why would I let my heart down?

May You be my Good Friend

May you be my Good Friend,
Celebrate to The End,
A star, a friend,
Know you are near.

Come together,
And all will mend.

Constantine

Eight-year-old Constantine wrote me a poem:

> "There was a boy called Jackson
> and he was a Prince
> and he met a girl
> who was a Princess.
>
> He was shocked by the girl
> she was beautiful.
> She thought he was stunning.
> He and the girl fell in love.
>
> They we King and Queen,
> so they got a castle
> and it was made out of gold
> so they celebrate a fest
> and had the best
> time of there lives,
> but then, they did the rong thing and
> spent all their money.
>
> The next morning they found out
> they didn't have any money
> so they sold their castle
> Then they were happy again.
> They lived happily ever after.
>
> The end."

Why not?!
I admire his plot.
It says a lot.

Today I Swim, Tomorrow I Dance

Twenty-seven and maybe in Heaven,
I opened the door and looked out to the seashore.

Where was I?
What have I accomplished?
Well, a series of "This" and "That"
And "Things" for chat,
But, how about my *Mustache Man*,
My *Knight in Shining Armor*?
That said, I waddle thru a few more…

It's not the quantity, I understand,
But, how comes he doesn't fit my hand?
Ok, I submit, I can take but maybe one more Kid,
Where is my Man?

I awaken again, bills piled high,
And only a fruit on my kitchen stand,
I eat it dearly, a peach with a seed, how clever indeed!
If we plant what we can, a new fruit will come,
But, where is my soil to lend me a hand?

Today I swim with another, and feel like a Queen,
Then, I come home and visit with my Enemy,
I need something more,
But cannot be what this person wants,
He's somewhat ok, but it doesn't go our way.

I open my Book, and read in the nook,
God willing, I end,
The passage makes me feel like a hen.
I do my cross, kiss my Book, and realize:
I'm thirty-four and maybe more!
It's hard to see Heaven again,
But maybe a scar from afar.

I wake up in sweat! I am swimming again,
The deep end is here, and I need something dear!
Why won't my questions be answered?
Can I come clear?

Today I swim, tomorrow I dance!
He's with me not by chance,
With a caring way and calm I have not known,
He understands God and brings from his small thrown.

He makes me feel tingly inside,
Why do I hesitate? How do I know?
I cannot decide because I have things to hide,
Instead I search for different, and don't see his side.

Gently ahead,
He moves on his own beat.
Climbing life's stormed mountain,
With blisters on his feet.
Courage at hand and worry may not be,
I want to say yes, but limit my calls and stay,
Fearing my leap.

Cleaning my home, I measure my grandmother's feet,
She's so grand, I live her defeat.
I love her so dearly,
And she gives me my glow.

I don't like the busy blues,
Why do I succumb?
Give me a chance,
For I'm not in slum!

My mother cries from her bed,
Worried and sad,
When will my daughter be settled and glad?
On that day, I see, it will be a great dance,
For I see a solution, so near and by happenstance.

He entered my life, to heal and to greet,
He is a great guy, so dear and complete.
So I opened my heart, and decided to see,
What may happen, if I let him meet my True Me.

We shared some time, as much as all day,
And, in that everlasting moment,
I felt something complete and to say.
Why did I not see clear, over the years we met?
This man, something dear, He is sweet I bet.

What waits for me in front,
I may not know,
But come close to my heart,
All will flow.

He's slipping away,
I hate to say.
I gave him a few glances,
But, I didn't know my chances.

Next, I must grasp his attention,
He's somewhere I know.
My calls go unanswered,
The cold winter He battles with snow.

What have I done?
Where is He now?
I know we are meant for another,
But, I didn't give him a vow.

Today, I received his letter,
He wrote me so dear.
I'm going to hold on,
I want him near.

My expenses and demands seem to be there for sure,
But I don't feel alone and in despair.
A help from a stranger, but yet He is mine,
We cuddle with love, and intertwine.

Today I may swim, but shallow waters are now here,
I enjoy the cool water with warm sunrays from There.
Tomorrow I dance, with a companion I love,
I'm with my Man, and a Paradise I see near.

Surprisingly, we really agree!
I capture the light, as I adore every night,
We are together,
And yet I am free!

And now I know,
Life is more than just for me,
It is to Love and cherish Jesus,
Yes, He.

One—A Haiku Poem

We are as two One
With my dame, God guides us thru
We live as One knew

Part 4.

The Life

A New Beginning

Love can only begin after
    I remove the child-like comments of:
        No…
            I don't know…
                Don't worry about it…
                    It doesn't matter.

These negatives strangle,
And hold unnecessary fear.

Better to deal with things,
As wrong as they may appear.

    And make,

        A New Beginning.

The Fifth Season

Bring forth the season's changes,
A gracious entrance of the Fifth season.
Have I forgotten who I am?
Review, respect, reflect—it is o.k.

It's time to see the new love,
Abundant and flowing throughout.
Not Winter, not Spring, but the season of Passion.
Born in transition, fulfilled with the triumphs of Spring
and the heat of Summer.

In enveloping into my soul,
Tonight listening gladly and holding
A warm yearning. I've eased.
Feel it coming, it's the Fifth season,
Between the first and second,
Who required sequence?

It is the heart that feels.
It is the mind that labels.
Placing you near, embracing your strength
And offering hand, I feel you.

It has filled the read,
I turn to my side
And pull you in.

We are one, in the Fifth Season.

Friends Pair with Intimacy

It was her eyes that first glanced,
That capturing smile returned genuine.
Joy and complete happiness
Maybe it was some Holiday madness!

It will be a friendship developed
And crossing paths at times,
That smile, an exchange, incredible
Brought hope to my sorrows.

Can I reach out and call,
But she may not respond,
A precious friend she is,
How awkward if she absconds.

At Sundance I swear, this Aphrodite I feel,
What man in this room would be strong for this bloom.
Esprit has its way and duty is few,
I stick to my course, thinking, maybe you.

I take it back a step
Impulse meet with a few,
She may be doing the same,
High spirits but none our cue.

Will I awaken joined next to her,
I dream for that moment élan view.
When life can gather my courage,
Viability her heart too.

Pleasant and noble, her name is but true,
Playful and dear, we are real and a match,
I'm not a Saint, but am I worthy for her?
Conceivably or I would hear a complaint.

Pairs never abandon, and tears can be licked,
Her kind gestures and moments of touch clicked,
It is perfectly made,
…A natural pair obeyed.

A sorbet we share and then I know,
She is a dream to me, free at last,
Capture her so, with kids, I know.
Sensibility is her cast,
Another night, I will make her glow!

That night came as friends we prepared,
Salmon and Caesar pair for dinner,
The Phantom of the Opera duo played strong,
And softly to passionately, we entered in song.

Amazing we feel,
Thoughtful and honest,
A good man and woman,
Embrace intimate thru.

I see her now, as I knew I would,
Enamored with her candid beauty
Friends paired with intimacy,
Brought to us and it is good.

Destination:
Life friends with affection,
Just as a couple should.

Soon, I See

Je cherche,
>Doux music to create with the.

A bit more,
>Come to the door adoration.

Soon, I see,
>A feeling of comfort to be.

Promise me,
>A kiss I want to mold with the.

Birds Without Wings

On the road thru Kabul, we travel Toyota strong.
My driver Hyamat approaches barricade wall twine.
Safety seems the force present,
But far from it he speeds then halts,
The ISAF and Embassy entrances difficult barricades.

Tomahawks align, blades tornado, gunners aim
It is the 4th of July, independence, though unnamed.

Actually, I notice an atmosphere of hardship and walls
Somehow, we make pleasure talk
We eat capers, salami and smoking cigars.
With my comrades, Lieutenant Stan and all.

The evening among Colonels, Generals, Captains, and Lieutenants
Makes me think about my freedom, simple and small.
I salute my colleagues, I am American proud,
But I have a hard time to holster gun or wear vest,
Even feel safer with no vest on my chest.

But the birds without wings clamber their size,
Huff, puff and time for a ride, helicopters surprise.
Only to return again bringing new birds without wings,
Stuck in an ugly nest.

I'm grateful for their presence and others too,
But what life to be caged behind walls, nothing new.
Like Hollywood or Vegas, garden mirages swell,
They may hide some blunders, flapping they try,
But who am I to question, as they protect us from hell.

Become

We fear those things we do not understand,
Challenge yourself to learn.
And you will become a stronger person.
Try. Inquire. Become.
Then, Lead.

We overhear prose wrings on the newsstand,
Scavenge thyself to turn.
And you nil welcome a babbler craftsman.
Pry. Atone. Schism.
So, Bleed.

We fear those things we do not understand,
Therefore, Become!

La Magie de Paris

Lumière, my light, my Parisienne magie,
Your eyes and personnage are magical.
Sophisticated and délicieux we met lovely,
Entering the café insured merriment intent.

Darling conversations we made,
Walking thru the promenade.
Hands clasped, we swayed along the provincial shops,
Chocolatiers, vêtements de bébé, livres et plus!

We took our time to listen and learn,
Each other holding turn.
At the café, suitable and sampling,
With wine glass we yearned.

I'm missing most of all, the memory of long for her,
Our welcome hearts pattering with blessings.
We chose chocolat noir together,
Holding hands, so agreeable like paintings.

You knew my scars, and listened with senses,
Always there, in your eyes and spiritual essence.
And when we kissed, fluid flowed,
Our passion engulfed, affectionate souls delighted.
Do you feel that? Can you hear it?
My heart beating for you, as our lips kissed,
We proclaimed devoted hours.
Your soft warm touch sent us and we knew,
Climbing those stairs as enchanted lovers.

T'adore! Lumière mon Parisienne magie,
I adore you, ma fleur!

A Theme not Twirled

A theme not twirled fair plans
No archer plans will mourn
Where love will bring you worth
And Greece's baths are worn.

A theme not twirled where all
Will slowly meet blossoms sway
Where greed will answer tax and toll
Nor Christmas lights our way.

Not twirled a theme scares back or bite
Believer face you see
'Till care the rallies of some worth
And angry clan is glee.

Where anchorless ill bang its dead
And boy, in a twirl,
Amends the seeds of brawl designed—
To touch a theme, so twirled.

Love captured a theme scared right or wrong
Brings forward chance to be strong
Where light and song deliver and show
Some boundless ties cut, but know.

Love Has No Scenery

Angelina Lambrini,
You are my definition of Love,
But when you grow, I want you to know…
Love is not what you may "Think" it to be.
First, it is important to be You,
But, love has no scenery.

There are no ideal relationships,
Just be candid, graceful and alive!
Soon you will be courted, and
Want flowers and romance to thrive.

These are the affairs of blushing Love,
But beware, a true love will be forever,
Like a father is to an heir.
True Love has no scenery,…it is bare.

You give it in small tasks,
In kindness and not from a flask.
A kiss on the forehead, a light touch on the hand,
May signify a kind heart, and offer of more,
Like millions of granules of sand.

It's not about romance alone,
But maybe a glimpse of life,
Love is found in…

- a family around a cemetery,
- a cup of hot chocolate,
- a smile or unknown friendly,
- a key to a home,
- but not a wallet!

Love has no scenery,
It is more than you know,
It appears in even a musical tone.

How lucky it is to have you,
A bundle of Love,
May always be true.
A feeling of safety and comfort,
Like Christmas each day, or
Food on the table made in a loving way.

Your heart may become empty,
And you may not see, but
Remember:

Love has no scenery.

Opa!

(I close with this, which may be the shortest poem ever written by a Greek. It signifies to Love Life! I hope you enjoyed the book. With love and affection, Nikos)

Opa!

About the Author

Nikos Linardakis grew up in Oak Brook, Illinois. As a writer, he worked in Chicago and New York, gathering themes from around the world of love, family, loss, hurt, healing and joy.

He published over a dozen books as past Editor-in-Chief with McGraw-Hill Companies in New York and with Gibbs-Smith Publishers. He has also written several articles and monographs as the Director of Clinical Research for The Natural Standard in Cambridge, Massachusetts, *El Mero*, and in the journal *Sleep & Health.*

Nikos attended Benedictine University with a degree in Biology, Masters of Science program in Applied Physiology and a Medical Doctorate from the University of Health Sciences/The Chicago Medical School.

His love of poetry has spanned his entire life, and began as a musician and bass guitarist, while he and his brothers' band first performed in Chicago in the early 1970's.

He is the father of three children and is fluent in English, Spanish and Greek languages, and learning Pashto.

LOVE, Poems of Longing is his first book of poetry.

www.ingramcontent.com/pod-product-compliance
Lightning Source LLC
Chambersburg PA
CBHW030003050426
42451CB00006B/97